BRANDING
3x3

How to build your brand in *simple* and *relatable steps*

By Clare Froggatt

Branding 3x3: How to build your brand in simple and relateable steps © Clare Froggatt 2022

The moral rights of Clare Froggatt to be identified as the author of this work have been asserted in accordance with the Copyright Act 1968.

ISBN: 9798840947654

Any opinions expressed in this work are exclusively those of the author. All rights reserved. No part of this publication may be reproduced or transmitted by any means, electronic, photocopying or otherwise, without prior written permission of the author.

Disclaimer

All the information, techniques, skills and concepts contained within this publication are of the nature of general comment only, and are not in any way recommended as individual advice. The intent is to offer a variety of information to provide a wider range of choices now and in the future, recognising that we all have widely diverse circumstances and viewpoints. Should any reader choose to make use of the information herein, this is their decision, and the author and publisher/s do not assume any responsibilities whatsoever under any conditions or circumstances. The author does not take responsibility for the business, financial, personal or other success, results or fulfillment upon the readers' decision to use this information. It is recommended that the reader obtain their own independent advice.

CONTENTS

FOREWORD
INTRODUCTION   7

BRAND STRATEGY
    - WHY – Your Brand Purpose   13
    - HOW – Your Values   17
    - WHAT – Your Mission   29

BRAND AUDIENCE
    - CHOOSING A TARGET AUDIENCE   41
    - CUSTOMER JOURNEY MAPPING   49
    - VALUE PROPOSITION   63

BRAND IDENTITY
    - LOGO   79
    - BRAND IDENTITY SYSTEM   85
    - CONSISTENCY IS KEY   89

NEED MORE HELP   105
GLOSSARY   107
THE AUTHOR   119
ACKNOWLEDGMENTS   121

SCAN ME

Clare Froggatt

FOREWORD

Branding 3x3 brings together the 'WHAT', 'WHY', and 'HOW' to create a brand for your business. The information is broken down into easy to follow steps and walks you through examples, with exercises to follow, so you can easily understand each concept and apply it to your business.

Most entrepreneurs, even experienced ones, build with the logo first and don't take into consideration the foundations or the customer journey.

If you follow this guide and think about your brand and how you communicate to your ideal customer then you will create a winning brand.

This book encompasses two decades of brand building experience across private and public sector organisations and a variety of industries .

Once you have worked through it, please send me a note. I would love to hear how this book helped you and your business to succeed.

INTRODUCTION

Branding is a very popular word in business but, what is it? What does it mean?

Quite frankly, it means a lot of different things to lots of people.

Some people think it's just your logo. It's not! Your logo is just a part of it. Like a jigsaw a brand is made up of many pieces, although your logo is the most recognisable part of it.

The 'M' from McDonald's (The Golden Arches); you can see a sign from miles away and you instantly know what it is. This makes your logo a pivotal part of you brand and your brand identity.

In this book I go through the three main elements of branding and the three key elements within each one.

If you work on putting the things I guide you through in this book in place and getting clarity, you won't have to worry so much about everything else. Concentrate on these elements, and everything else sort of comes along with it.

Think of an iceberg. Above the water you have your logo, your social media, website, and the customer experience you provide – these are the tangible assets of your brand that provide the tools for you to promote your business and offer. Below the water is the strategy, your purpose, mission, values, customer journey... the map that provides the direction and reason.

This Branding 3x3 Playbook will help you understand and build your brand by mapping that direction and reason . From the strategy that will guide your business growth to delivering a brand identity that resonates with your ideal customer, to implementing the strategies into your own business.

All the elements shown in the Iceberg model can be overwhelming, so I have developed this framework that covers the three main parts of a brand and the three key elements within them.

If you work on putting these things in place, and getting clarity, you won't have to worry so much about everything else. Concentrate on these elements, and everything else sort of comes along with it.

The three main areas are your:
- Brand Strategy
- Your Audience
- Brand Identity

Strategy - who you are? what do you do? who do you do it for? and why do you do it?

What gets you out of bed in the morning, beyond making money?

Audience - who are your customers? Because if you haven't got any customers, you haven't got a business.

Identity - your logo and all tangible tools you have, the visual things, maybe the audio things, video, and podcasts - they are all a part of your brand identity.

Whether you are launching a start-up, growing an established business, or starting a rock band, The Branding 3x3 Playbook will help you succeed in your market.

You can't build a reputation on what you are going to do.
    Henry Ford

01
02
03

BRAND STRATEGY

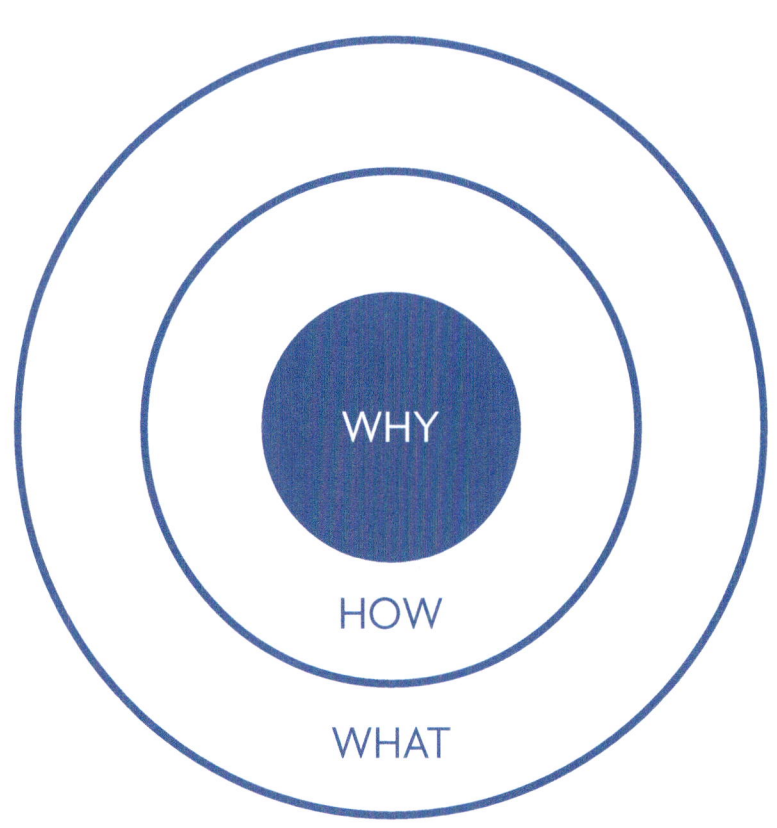

WHY – Your Brand Purpose

Every one of us has a WHY. A deep-seated purpose, cause or belief that is the source of our passion and inspiration.

How we feel about something or someone is more powerful than what we think about it or them. Communicating our feelings is hard so we often resort to metaphors like "I feel like a kid in a playground again". When we emotionally align with our customers and customers the payoff is huge, our **connection** is much **stronger** and more **meaningful** than any affiliation based on features or benefits.

Knowing the deeper 'WHY' your company or brand exists provides the **foundation** on which to build everything else — your 'HOW' and your 'WHAT'.

A brand's purpose is essentially a brand's reason for being, beyond making money. It's important to not confuse this with a 'brand promise'. A brand promise may give the buyer an idea of what to expect from the product or service, but the brand purpose goes way beyond that.

A brand purpose **connects** with customers on a more emotional level.

HOW TO DEVELOP YOUR BRAND PURPOSE?
1. Be clear about what your brand is, who it's for and why you do what you do
2. Think long term
3. Put your customer first
4. Bring everything together into a short, simple and, most importantly, genuine message
5. Once you find it, make it stick

HERE'S SOME "WHY" AND "WHAT" QUESTIONS TO ASK
This will help you **focus** on what matters most about working at or in your business. Consider questions such as:

- Why are we doing this?
- Why are we in business?
- Why do we exist?
- Why are we who we are today?
- Why are we good at what we do?
- What do people say about us?
- What are we great at?

HERE ARE SOME GOOD BRAND PURPOSE EXAMPLES

A succinct, well-articulated brand purpose that everyone in the business knows and believes in is crucial.

Nike: "To bring inspiration and innovation to every athlete in the world. If you have a body, you are an athlete."

Crayola: "Encouraging children to be creative, and enabling parents to inspire them"

Google: "To organize the world's information and make it universally accessible and useful."

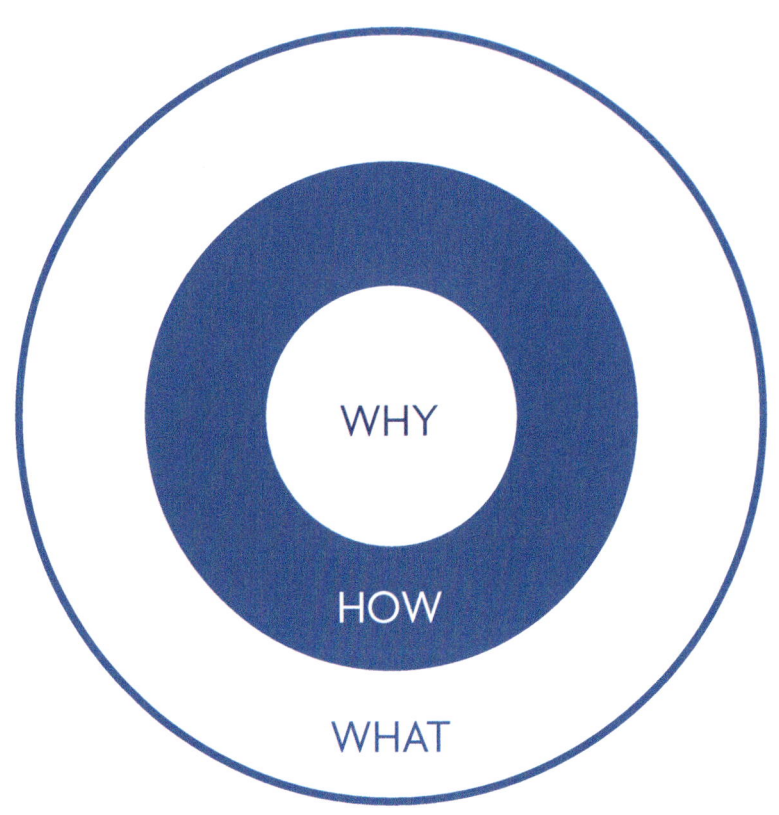

HOW – Your Values

What are Brand Values?
Core brand values are the beliefs that you, as a business, stand for.

They are how you communicate the attributes you find most important and are the driving force that guides every decision you make with your branding. Unlike your aims which define the things you hope your business will achieve; your brand values are more like **promises for how your business will conduct itself**.

Choosing **authentic** and strong core brand values can help you to set your business apart from others in the same industry. They'll also allow you to develop **meaningful relationships** with your customers and can be even more important than having the best product or service available. **Communicating** your brand values well will help you to attract your ideal customers, and people who share your values are also more likely to become loyal to your brand.

HOW TO DEFINE CLEAR BRAND VALUES FOR YOUR BUSINESS
In a world where people are constantly looking for connections with their favourite brands, it's crucial for companies to give their **customers** something that they can **relate** to, that goes beyond a beautiful logo or an impressive website.

Brand values are such a key part of developing a strong brand, let's dive into what your brand values are all about and how you can define core brand values that:

- Are genuine and true to your business
- Help you connect with your ideal customers
- And set you apart from the competition

GO BEYOND THE OBVIOUS
When it comes to defining your brand values, you might start with words like "**trust**" or "**heart**" or "**reliability**". While there's nothing wrong with these values, it's also important to think of how you can make these values more characteristic of your unique business. On their own, these kinds of values don't do much to **set you apart**. Instead, they sound like generic values that every business stands for at a bare minimum.

Instead, consider how you can be a little more **specific** to your niche or industry. Think about what kind of experience your ideal customers are looking for, when choosing a business to go to. What are some negative aspects of your industry, that your business specifically overcomes?

BE AUTHENTIC, TO BE UNIQUE

The best way to set your business apart and find a way to be unique is to make sure you're being authentic. Ask yourself:

- What does my business stand for?
- When conducting my business, what do I consider most important?
- What do I believe in?

By working out **why your business exists**, you'll discover values that clearly explain why you do what you do, and how it helps your ideal market. Set a **standard of behaviour** for your business and stick to it. Your brand values are promises to your customers about what they can expect from you.

The brand values you define should be values that are naturally infused into your everyday practices and the way you run your business. If they aren't, then the values you've chosen are not a real representation of the things you truly find important. If your business says it values one thing and then behaves in a way that goes against those values, that creates a dishonest image. You're not too likely to attract loyal customers this way.

On the other hand, if your brand values are a real representation of what you believe in as a business, then they become a **strong part of your story and brand**. This helps your business to make a stand and stand out.

STUCK? THINK ABOUT THE NEGATIVE
If you're struggling to specify the things you find important as a business, then it might help you consider the negative aspects of your industry. What are some of the typical downsides that your ideal customers face when trying to find or use the product or service you offer? What obstacles do they have to deal with? Maybe it's confusion about the steps they need to take to order a product. Or they might be concerned about a lack of communication between them and their service provider. Perhaps timing is a big issue for them?

Then, think about how your business overcomes those negatives. What problem does your business have a **solution** to that you can highlight as a **massive positive** to **your ideal customer**s? How do you reassure them that your business is the right choice to make

COMMUNICATE YOUR BRAND VALUES
Once you know your values (and don't go overboard with them — I advise sticking to three!) then you want to let your audience know what they are. Use your brand values to attract your ideal customers. Use them as a **selling point**. Use them to maintain a highly consistent brand that strongly communicates what your business is all about.

You should also incorporate your brand values into the way you introduce your business. Don't just state what you do. Explain why! This makes your business more **memorable** and **meaningful**. It's the difference between, "I build lead-generating websites" and "I make it possible for business to grow exponentially by building lead-generating websites".

BRAND VALUES CEMENT RELATIONSHIPS

To some extent, finding the answer to the question "What are brand values?" means looking at your brand as a whole. Most brands consist of a range of "external" assets, including a verbal identity, which outlines your **tone of voice and personality**, and your visual identity, which includes logos, colours, and fonts.

It's the "internal" part of your brand that truly transforms the relationships you build with your customers. That internal element is your "brand values", the part of your marketing mix that **guides your purpose, personality**, and **proposition**.

While both of these elements can **help to establish brand loyalty** by creating **feelings** of **familiarity** and **affinity**, without a brand value proposition, you can't differentiate your company from your competitors, and as we all know, it's the memorable brand**s** that win the most customers. Core brand values, along with your fine-tuned brand communication strategy, helps shape the culture and community of your brand, ensuring that you **connect** with your **customers** in a meaningful way.

ANY BRAND VALUES DEFINITION SHOULD BE:

- **Memorable:** Brand values do not mean much if they are not constantly represented by the things you do and say. Your customers and employees need to be able to remember your beliefs if you want them to have an impact.

- **Unique:** This is something that goes without saying, but your brand values definition should be a unique reflection of your culture and identity. You can't simply copy and paste something that works for another business. Look at strong companies for inspiration, but make sure your core values represent your company DNA.

- **Actionable:** Your brand value proposition is something that needs to guide how your business works. When defining what matters to your company, choose actionable language. For instance, don't just say you "value integrity". Tell your customers that you work to do the right thing and describe how you do that.

- **Meaningful:** Empty phrases that look as though they've been picked at random from a dictionary won't do anything for your business. If you want your core brand values to resonate with your customers, they need to include things you're willing to fight for.

- **Clear and defined:** Vague and value are two terms that rarely go together. When choosing the principles on which to build your brand, make sure that the things you stand for are easy to understand. For example, Netflix has a slideshow describing what each of their values means.

- **Timeless:** While companies and customers can change with time – your brand values should remain consistent and strong. They can bend and grow with you over the years, but make sure you maintain consistency.

> MY OWN EXAMPLE
>
> One of my core brand values is "building relationships". It's a concept that's central to my approach to branding, and something I put a lot of emphasis on in my own business. As a solo business owner, I always work directly with my customers, at every step of their branding process. I'm the one who consults with them, develops their brand strategy and brings their identity design to life. There's no passing any of the work onto an unknown team member or outsourcing it.
>
> It's something I use as a selling point. Something that sets me apart from branding agencies where the person speaking directly to the customer isn't necessarily the same person who develops the designs or comes up with concepts.
>
> I don't think there's anything wrong with the way branding agencies do their work. It's simply different than the way I run my business and I choose to point this out as a positive aspect of working with me. Doing so helps me to attract the kind of customers who prefer working this way.
>
> When you choose your core brand values, make sure you're highlighting values that showcase how and why they're important to you and your customers.

HOW TO CHOOSE YOUR VALUES AND INTEGRATE THEM INTO YOUR MESSAGING

Five steps to choosing your values and integrating them into your messaging so, you can attract ideal customers.

Step 1: Start with a brain dump
Let it all out. List a bunch of words or short phrases that describe the values that are important to you. Attributes that describe your brand culture. The things you stand for. Reasons why your target market would choose your business over others.

At this point, we're not looking for quality. Just a free-flowing brainstorm of ideas that lead to other ideas. Keep going until you have a decent size list. Maybe 15-20 words.

Step 2: Cull your list
Cut out the noise. Trying to focus on too many values will dilute your message and lessen its impact. Instead, highlight two–four of your strongest values that will act as the pillars of your brand.

These values should describe what you actively stand for — what you believe in and practice now, rather than how you aspire to be or are reaching towards (this isn't your brand vision we're creating here)

Step 3: Expand on your chosen words
A word on its own doesn't say much. So, use a sentence or two to explain what each of your selected words/phrases really means for your business.

If your brand values could also describe every other business in your industry, you need to **dig a little deeper**. Remember that the point of branding is differentiation.

Step 4: Consider how you demonstrate these values
Think of the ways you actually showcase your chosen values in what you do and the way you do it. If the brand values you've chosen are a true representation of what you genuinely stand for, they should already be naturally integrated into the way you run your business. This could be in how you approach customer service, or the way you package your offers.

List examples of how these values influence the way you choose to grow and develop your business and the way they impact the quality of the services you deliver. Your **ideal customers** likely share these same values. How do you make sure you're **meeting their expectations** and delivering on your **promises** to them?

Step 5: Create examples of messaging that communicate your values
Don't hide your brand values or simply throw them onto your website's "about" page, never to be of any use to anyone. Your brand values are an important way to connect with your ideal customers and as such, should be at the front of all your messaging.

This means they should come through in the way your brand speaks. Phrase your values in a way that highlights the benefit to your customers. Instead of "**time-efficient**", you can say you "**I help save you hours of research**". Let your customers know how your values help them.

SOME EXAMPLES OF CORE VALUES

- A commitment to **sustainability** and to acting in an **environmentally friendly** way. Companies like Patagonia and Ben & Jerry's have environmental sustainability as a core value.

- A commitment to **innovation** and **excellence**. Apple Computer is perhaps best known for having a commitment to innovation as a core value. This is embodied by their "Think Different" motto.

- A commitment to **doing good for the whole**. Google, for example, believes in making a great search engine and building a great company without being evil.

- A commitment to **helping those less fortunate**. TOMS shoe company gives away a pair of shoes to a needy person for every pair it sells to alleviate poverty and make life better for others.

- A commitment to **building strong communitie**s. Shell oil company donates millions of dollars to the University of Texas to improve student education and to match employee charitable donations.

THE BRAND VALUES EXAMPLE LIST

Abundance	Discretion	Harmony	Popularity
Acceptance	Diversity	Health	Positivity
Accessibility	Dreams	Heart	Potential
Accountability	Drive	Heroism	Power
Accuracy	Duty	History	Precision
Activeness	Eagerness	Honesty	Pride
Adaptability	Ease of use	Honour	Privacy
Adventure	Economy	Hope	Productivity
Affection	Education	Humility	Professionalism
Ambition	Effectiveness	Humour	Progress
Appreciation	Elegance	Imagination	Purity
Approachability	Empathy	Impact	Quality
Attention to detail	Empowering	Individuality	Recognition
Balance	Energy	Innovation	Reflection
Beauty	Engagement	Insight	Relationships
Belonging	Enjoyment	Inspiration	Reliability
Bravery	Entertainment	Integrity	Resilience
Capability	Enthusiasm	Intelligence	Resourcefulness
Care	Entrepreneurship	Intimacy	Respect
Change	Environment	Intuition	Responsibility
Charity	Equality	Joy	Safety
Clarity	Evolution	Justice	Satisfaction
Cleanliness	Excellence	Kindness	Security
Collaboration	Excitement	Knowledge	Sharing
Comfort	Exhilaration	Leadership	Simplicity
Commitment	Expertise	Learning	Sincerity
Communication	Exploration	Liveliness	Skill
Compassion	Fairness	Logic	Speed
Confidence	Faith	Longevity	Spontaneity
Connection	Family	Love	Stability
Consistency	Fame	Loyalty	Strength
Control	Fascination	Mastery	Success
Cooperation	Fearlessness	Mindfulness	Support
Courage	Firmness	Motivation	Sustainability
Craftiness	Fitness	Neatness	Talent
Craftsmanship	Flexibility	Optimism	Teamwork
Creativity	Focus	Organisation	Thoughtfulness
Credibility	Freedom	Originality	Tolerance
Curiosity	Freshness	Partnership	Trust
Customer-centric	Friendship	Passion	Truth
Daring	Fun	Patience	Understanding
Dedication	Generosity	Peace	Uniqueness
Dependability	Genius	Perception	Unity
Determination	Genuineness	Performance	Value
Devotion	Goodwill	Persistence	Variety
Dignity	Gratitude	Personal development	Virtue
Diligence	Growth	Playfulness	Vision
Directness	Guidance	Poise	Warmth
Discipline	Happiness	Polish	Welcoming
Discovery	Hard work		Wonder

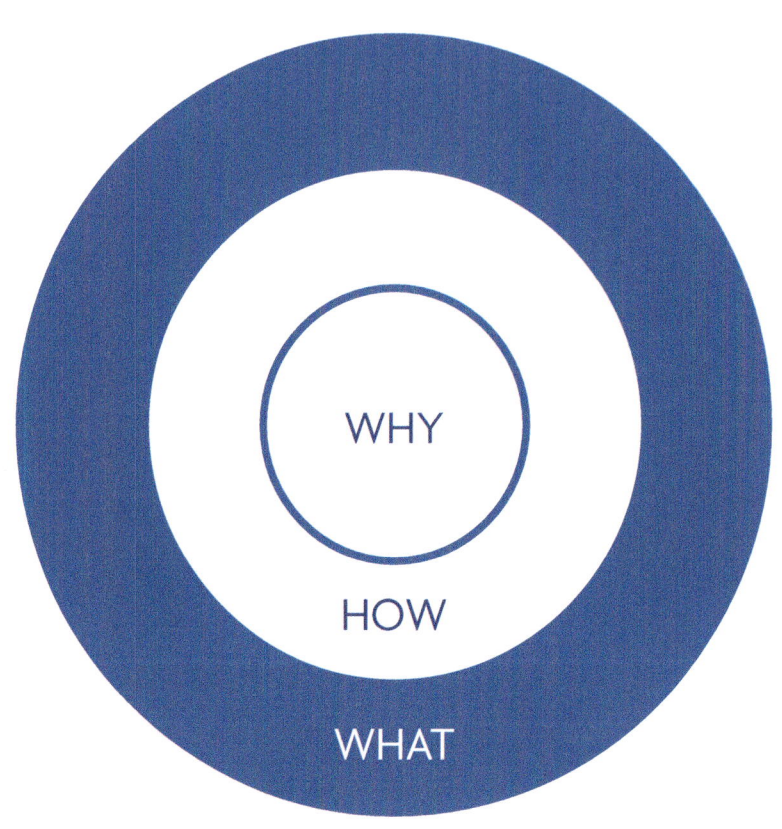

WHAT – Your Mission

WHAT IS BRAND MISSION?

A mission statement is a simple statement that explains your company's goals. It's a summary of what your company does for its **customers**, **employees**, and **owners**. It explains how you do what you do. And, it focuses on why your company does what it does.

Developing your company's first mission statement, or writing a new or revised one, is your opportunity to **define the company's goals, ethics, culture**, and **norms** for **decision-making**.

HOW TO WRITE A GREAT MISSION STATEMENT

So, how do you make a great mission statement? Over the decades I've spent reading, writing, and evaluating strategic plans, I've come up with a process for developing a useful mission statement, and it boils down to five steps.

Step 1: Start with a defining story

A really good defining story explains the need, or the want, or—if you like jargon—the so-called "why to buy". It defines the target customer or "buyer persona". It defines how your business is different from most others, or even unique. It simplifies thinking about what a business isn't, what it doesn't do.

Step 2: Define what your business does for its customers

Start your mission statement with the **good you do**. Use your market-defining story to work out whatever it is that makes your business special for your target customer.

Step 3: Define what your business does for its employees

Good businesses are good for their employees too or they don't last. Keeping employees is better for the bottom line than turnover. Company culture matters. **Rewarding** and **motivating people** matters. A mission statement can define what your business offers its employees.

Qualities like fairness, diversity, respect for ideas and creativity, training, tools, empowerment, and the like, actually **really matter**. However, since every business in existence at least says that it prioritizes those things, strive for a **differentiator** and a way to make the general goals feel more concrete and specific.

Step 4: Add what the business does for its owners
Generally speaking, it is thought that the mission of management is to enhance the value of the stock. And shares of stock are ownership. Some would say that it goes without saying that a business exists to enhance the financial position of its owners...

However, only a few businesses are about "share value" and "return on investment."

Step 5: Discuss, digest, cut, polish, review, revise
Whatever you wrote for points two to four above, go back and cut down the wordiness.

Good mission statements serve multiple functions, define objectives, and live for a long time. **So edit**. This step is worth it.

Quality questions create a quality life. Successful people ask better questions, and as a result they get better answers.

——— Tony Robbins

QUESTIONS TO ASK...

Ask yourself the following questions to help develop your mission statement:

- What do we do?
- Why did I go into business in the first place?
- Or, if you're not a founder of the business... Why did I want to work at this company/in this industry?
- What do I want this company's legacy to be?
- What doesn't matter to this company's legacy?
- How do I want to help people?
- What value does our company bring that's unique from other companies?

Remember, your mission statement isn't set in stone. It's actually wise to **revisit** your mission statement once in a while to see if it still aligns with your company's goals. Some companies, for example, choose to write mission statements that help them solve a short-term problem their company is facing – these can be updated later to reflect a larger mission once your short-term issues are addressed.

.

BRAND MISSION STATEMENT FORMULA

Use the simple formula below to write a short mission statement for Brand Mission statement.

> At [COMPANY NAME], it's our mission to help [TARGET CUSTOMER] do / achieve / reach / eliminate / reduce [HAPPINESS/PAIN] by providing [A BENEFICIAL OUTCOME].

Let's break it down:
This one is pretty obvious, because it's the name of your company. If you don't have a name, use Acme as a placeholder.

Target Customer:
These are the users of your product or service. Picture your ideal customers. Describe the group in detail with a phrase like, "frazzled university professors." Doing this helps your potential users identify themselves right away.

Do/Achieve/Reach/Eliminate/Reduce + Happiness or Pain:
There are two primary ways your product or service affects your customers. You either increase their happiness, or you reduce their pain.

Ask yourself:
What does my company help people do or stop doing? Think about how current customers describe your company. What do they say? How did you help them? Did you save them time, make things easier etc. Make note of things like this.

Beneficial Outcome:
Think about the biggest benefit you promise will happen as a result of using your product or service. This is a strong way to end your mission statement. If you're not sure about the benefits, again, listen to your customers. They'll be happy to tell you.

Now, let's a look at the formula once it's pieced together:

"At Acme, it's our mission to help frazzled university professors reduce the time they spend hunched over handwritten records, calculating grades by providing easy-to-use apps that transform student performance data into gorgeous info graphics."

BRAND MISSION STATEMENT EXAMPLES

AirBnB

AirBnb describes its mission as, "For so long, people thought Airbnb was about renting houses. But really, we're about home. You see, a house is just a space, but a home is where you belong. And what makes this global community so special is that for the very first time, you can belong anywhere. That is the idea at the core of our company: belonging".

Amazon

From the Amazon Fact sheet, "To be Earth's most customer-centric company where people can find and discover anything they want to buy online."

Amazon expands on this as follows:

"This goal continues today, but Amazon's customers are worldwide now, and have grown to include millions of Customers, Sellers, Content Creators, and Developers & Enterprises. Each of these groups has different needs, and we always work to meet those needs, innovating new solutions to make things easier, faster, better, and more cost-effective."

Facebook

Facebook's mission is: "To give people the power to build community and bring the world closer together. People use Facebook to stay connected with friends and family, to discover what's going on in the world, and to share and express what matters to them".

> What you get by achieving your goals is not as important as what you become by achieving your goals.

— Zig Ziglar

01
02
03

YOUR AUDIENCE

> Your brand is what other people say about you when you are not in the room

— Jeff Bezos

BRAND AUDIENCE

CHOOSING A TARGET AUDIENCE

Unfortunately, no matter how innovative or world-changing your product or service might be, it's not going to appeal to everyone.

You might launch your bakery store thinking that you'll target everyone who's hungry. However, whilst a lot of people like cake, there are individuals out there that don't like sweets, have various allergies, or are on a diet (and therefore avoiding cake).

Designing a target audience means figuring out **who** is most likely to **buy** your product and why.

So, ask yourself:
- Who is my customer?
- What pain points do they have?
- What are their goals?

CREATE AND DESIGN PRODUCTS AND SERVICES YOUR IDEAL CUSTOMER WILL WANT TO BUY.

Use what you've learned to create new products, tweak existing ones, or to add new services to your portfolio.

For example, if you're a fitness coach and have found through your research that your ideal customer struggles with meal planning, you can **tailor your offerings** to this need.

Some ideas for how to do this: a customised meal planning service, an eBook with healthy recipes, a downloadable guide to planning and cooking an entire month of meals in one afternoon, etc.

MARKET YOUR STUFF USING WHAT YOU'VE LEARNED

Your research should have revealed where your target audience hangs out online, and what types of marketing content they prefer. This will help you streamline your marketing efforts, giving you the best chance of reaching your target market.

For instance, if you **know your ideal customer** is mainly on Facebook, you can focus more of your efforts there.

Or, if you've discovered their preference is for video over text or image, you can create video ads rather than wasting all your time on text ads.

> Everyone is not your customer

——— Seth Godin

IDEAL CUSTOMER PROFILE

By knowing who your ideal customer is you can **create targeted marketing messaging** directly towards them. The benefit of this is they will feel like you are speaking directly to them, you understand their pains and can help them.

Don't worry about focusing in one type of person or group of people you will still attract other people – it works like **throwing a pebble in a pond** – the more targeted you are the easier it is to aim but the ripples will reach further.

Your ideal customer(s) **(you can have more than one** for your different products or services, I have three.

Think about your existing customer base. Which customers do you love, which ones are the most profitable, who has the same values and is a dream to work with as you are on the same wavelength.

The term '**ideal customer**' is used to describe the one person that you want to do business with. Imagine that you are creating a social media post or free download for your website to attract and appeal to your ideal customer.

How would you describe them?

What are the qualities of your ideal customer? Why are current customers likely to buy your new product?

Remember to consider these three things when defining your ideal customer:
- Age
- Gender
- Location

Think about each of their **actions, motivations, questions,** and your **opportunities** to help them **solve their problem** or improve their situation.

Give them a name and a face – find stock image or picture your best customer

DESCRIBE YOUR IDEAL CUSTOMER IN DETAIL:

Age	Location

Gender	Income level

Education level	Occupation

Marital / Family status

Personality, Attitudes, Values

Interests / Hobbies

How does your product or service fit into your target customer's lifestyle?

How and when will your target customer use the product or service?

What features are most appealing to your target customer?

What media does your customer turn to for info? (Example: newspaper, blogs or online, events)

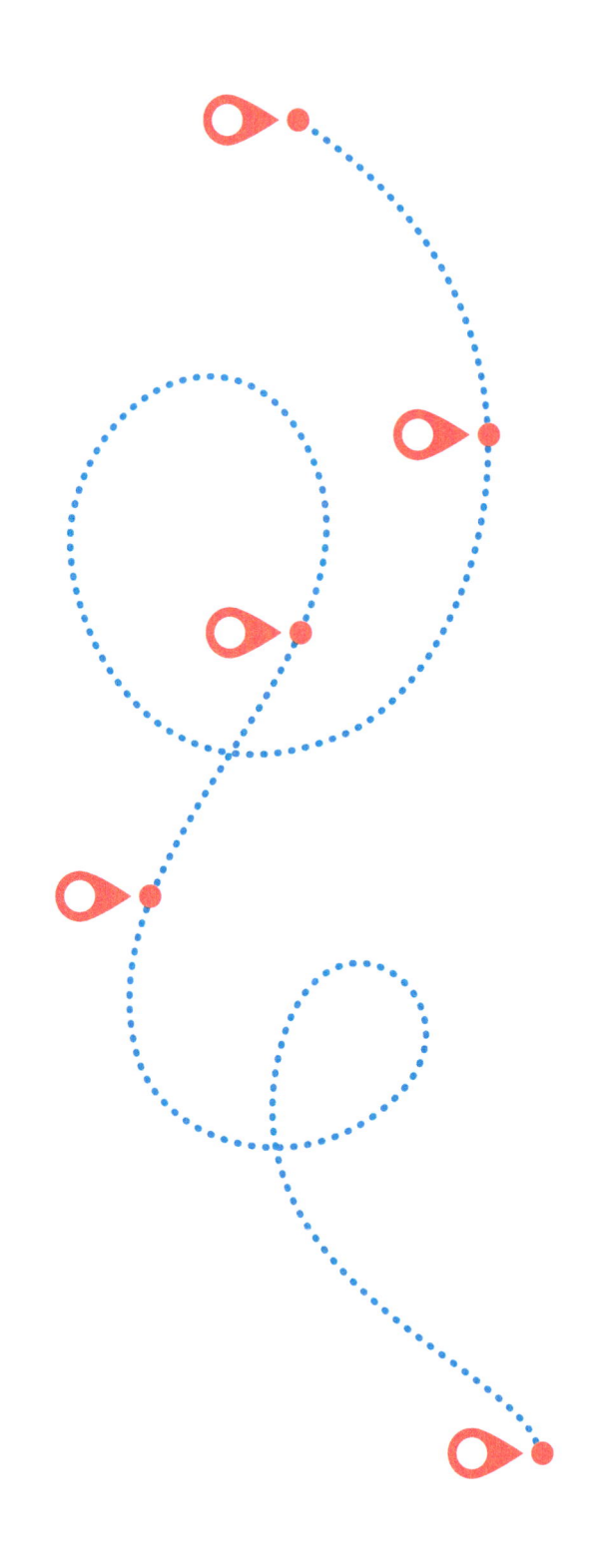

CUSTOMER JOURNEY MAPPING

Think about your business from your customers point of view, when doing this it helps to put yourself in their shoes – we are all customers, and we know what we want and how we like to be treated.

Imagine you are a customer of your own business, what is the journey, how many touch points are there from finding you to contacting you, making a purchase, delivery, and after care?

If thinking about the whole process in one go seems overwhelming **focus on each part of your customer's journey** in turn and include the following stages:

Awareness – the customer is seeking a solution to a problem
Consideration – the customer knows about you and is considering your offering
Purchase – the transaction takes place
Service – the experience the customer has with you
Loyalty – repeat business and referrals and recommendations

Look at each point of contact, ownership of those touch points, and the objective of each of them from the point of view of both the customer and the business.

Take your customers from a cold lead who is just discovering your company, right through their experience with you, to the point of becoming an ambassador for your company and telling others about you.

AWARENESS

The Awareness stage is often the stage that business owners consider the most and involves the most **marketing and sales effort**. Ultimately this is where customers find out about you or your product.

This is the fact-finding stage and where your social media and website will be checked, along with reviews and any other marketing you have out there. This is the "**Googling**" stage of the process. During this stage aim to **capture** as much **information** as possible.

Knowing your customers, having a customer avatar (ideal customer profile) and **answering** your **customers' pain points** are all things that can help you to map this section of the journey successfully.

Now you know that your customer is looking for **information** during this stage, that's exactly what you'll want to **provide** for them in a digestible format that's simple and very easy for them to find.

Content to Deliver in the Awareness Stage:
- How-to's
- White paper
- Industry reports
- eBooks
- Checklist
- How-to video

CONSIDERATION

Consideration is the second stage of the Customer Journey. By now your potential customer has done some basic research and is looking for someone who can help them to **solve the problem** that they have, they are looking for someone just like you!

At this stage the customer is ready to decide who they want to work with, they will be looking for more in-depth information than in the last stage and you need to position this in a way that convinces them to work with you. You need to **discuss your USPs, show proof** and answer the question, **why you?**

At this stage in the journey, actions have moved more towards structured research. People are now looking for specific information to help them make a **decision**, alongside specific online searches they will also be asking colleagues and their wider network for **recommendations**.

People will also be looking for proof and **validation of expertise** such as testimonials, awards, and accreditations. These need to be easy to find and well promoted. Professional accreditations are great but so are other awards such as peer recognition and both local and national awards.

Not only this but **showing people** you are also valued as an expert through the workshops, masterminds, and webinars that you have coming up and have previously delivered can also be a huge differentiator when positioned correctly at this stage.

Motivations will have also slightly altered at this stage of the journey. In Awareness people were looking for where to go and how to get support but now they are aware of what they need and are actively **looking for someone who can help**. They have become more critical of who the experts are, alongside if they can and should be trusted. They are looking more closely into the business that they are **considering**, to check if they actually can **deliver** what they promise to.

It's time to show up and shine!

Business owners considering you as a supplier also want to know and understand the following key questions,

- What happens next?
- How can they best contact you?
- What will working with you involve?
- What does an average project look like and how long will this take?
- What can they expect from a cost perspective and how can this fit into their cash flow.

Answering these questions **openly** and in **advance** will enable you to keep things moving and although you provide all of this information when you conduct meetings to discuss the project, discussing within FAQs or on your website or even via video may encourage more people to contact you to book meetings, as these questions will be answered in advance, again **building trust** with you.

People in the Consideration stage want to have their **individual needs** met and feel in control of the situation. For most businesses, this involves meetings and narrowing the search down to three or four main companies each of which will offer them what they need and want "on paper".

They are now looking to find out if any of these would be a good fit for them and are more than likely to invite these potential providers/ partners in for a meeting to pitch themselves and their offering.

Consideration means **doing all you can** to get your business shortlisted as one of the three that will be invited for a meeting and making sure that this meeting is a **success**.

Think about:
- Why you?
- Capturing information
- Make it easy for them to buy from you
- The numbers
- The follow-up
- Lead nurturing
- The opportunity

Often, it's during the Consideration stage that prospective buyers will reach out for more information by entering their information through one of your forms, calling the number on your website, or engaging on your social media channels. If this is happening, **do NOT leave them hanging**.

Content to Deliver in the Consideration Stage:
- Product webinar
- Case study
- Sample
- FAQ
- Data sheet
- Demo video

PURCHASE

At this point of the journey, a prospective customer is ready to become a paying customer. Making the purchase as simple as possible will go a long way. There are still lots of opportunities here to **enhance the journey** a prospective customer takes with you through effective follow-up and positioning.

Look at your proposals, quotes, received purchase orders, how you **keep in contact** with new customers in the early days and how you can create an **amazing experience**.

Agreeing on Payment with your customers - Making it easy
This is a very simple and effective process, one that makes purchasing with you easy. This is a huge benefit when choosing a supplier of any kind and maybe something to talk about in your proposal when it can be a differentiator.

Payment Options
Do you offer multiple payment methods such as Card (Credit card or Debit Card) or Bank Transfer, PayPal or Stripe or can you offer Direct Debit. Or do you just take cash?

Payment Terms
The ability to offer multiple payment terms means that you can offer your services to a wider range of businesses.

The Welcome pack and On boarding

How you welcome people as customers is something people remember and it sets the tone for the entire relationship. This is a great opportunity to give value-added information and **set the tone and expectations** for your continued working relationship. It also gives people something they can refer back to when needed and can avoid unnecessary questions.

Content to Deliver in the Decision Stage:
- Customer reviews
- Case studies
- Free trial
- Live demo
- Consultation
- Coupon

SERVICE

When it comes to the Service stage of the journey, think about the **service that you deliver** and the level of customer service that is delivered alongside each interaction that you have with a customer after they make the initial purchase with you.

Communications
Communicate clearly and regularly about product and service delivery stages, **notify of any issues or delays**.

Up sell and cross sell opportunities
Keeping in touch with your customers will allow you to **spot opportunities** where they might need more help or other products, or services from you.

Ongoing communications
It's far easier and roughly **ten times cheaper** to retain an existing customer than it is to acquire a new one. It's hard to build enough trust with a prospect to turn them into a first-time buyer, so once you've gained their trust and their business, you should be working hard to maintain it. During this stage you should be **following up** with your customer to get their **feedback** on the product or service that they purchased from you.

Account management
Account management is something that can help you to deliver a positive customer experience and also help you to identify potential opportunities for future work.

Aim to complete all account management calls once per quarter. The thought behind this is that the perceived randomness of these calls mean your customers feel you have just been thinking about them and have decided to call them, as opposed to this being a monthly scheduled call.

I would advise the following aim for each call either the customer is available to speak there and then, you schedule a time and date that is more convenient for them, or you leave them a voicemail letting them know you called and that you would love to hear from them.

Ideally, you want 3-4 key points to discuss on these calls could include the following;
- How are they?
- How is their business?
- Has anything changed since the last time you spoke that you can tell them about?
- Do you have any events coming up in your calendar to invite them to?
- Can you offer any additional support to them at the moment?
- Did they know you have XYZ offer/ event etc coming up or
- Have they seen XYZ in your Facebook group as you would love their feedback/ thoughts?

Content to Deliver in the Retention Stage:
- Service surveys
- Testimonial requests
- Follow up satisfaction phone calls
- How to's on using your product or service

LOYALTY

Loyalty is the final stage of the customer journey and it's where you focus on building loyalty, whether that be for **repeat business** or **referrals** and **recommendations**. Focus on how you can best ask for these and how you can best utilize these once they have been received.

Customers who stay with us long term are more profitable and are more likely to refer, recommend and review us and our businesses so getting this right is important.

Rewarding Loyalty

The first stage of building loyalty is **thanking your customers** in some way for doing business with you, this could be a video message, and email or a handwritten branded thank you card.

Launching a VIP program for existing customers is a great way to build further loyalty, this way your existing customers receive further benefits.

The **VIP customers** could have access to your diary before anyone else, by sending them emails letting them know that you are opening your diary for the year, for the season or quarter, people will **feel important** and that they have **priority**, which they do. Making them feel special and further **establishing the relationship** that they have with you and building additional loyalty.

Reviews, Testimonials and Case Studies

The best way to collect testimonials is just to ask! If users are satisfied with your services, chances are they'll be happy to talk about them. You can do this via phone call or email.

You could add a Google review or Trustpilot link to your invoice template or email signature, then you don't have to think about sending it out.

I have a link in the message that goes out with my electronic invoices that says "If you are happy with the service and results we have delivered and haven't left a review yet – please leave one here..." Adding the Google review link.

Making things easy for people makes them more likely to do something.

Here are some prompts you might want to send your users to incorporate into their testimonials:
- What are their favourite features?
- What was their business life like before using your product vs. after?
- How is your product helping them grow?

Case studies are also useful, these are generally longer format and are solution driven and relatable.

Referrals, Partnerships and Collaboration
The key to receiving a good referral is the timing and this is something that can be hard to judge. I believe that you should ask for a referral when **your customer is at their happiest**. This may be at different stages of the project so, given this, you should have a **process** to ensure that you ask everyone you work with and that this is not missed as part of the process. Adding this into your final **follow-up** would be a quick and simple way to do this if there is not a natural opportunity to do so before this point.

> **Make a customer not a sale**
>
> —— Anon

BRAND

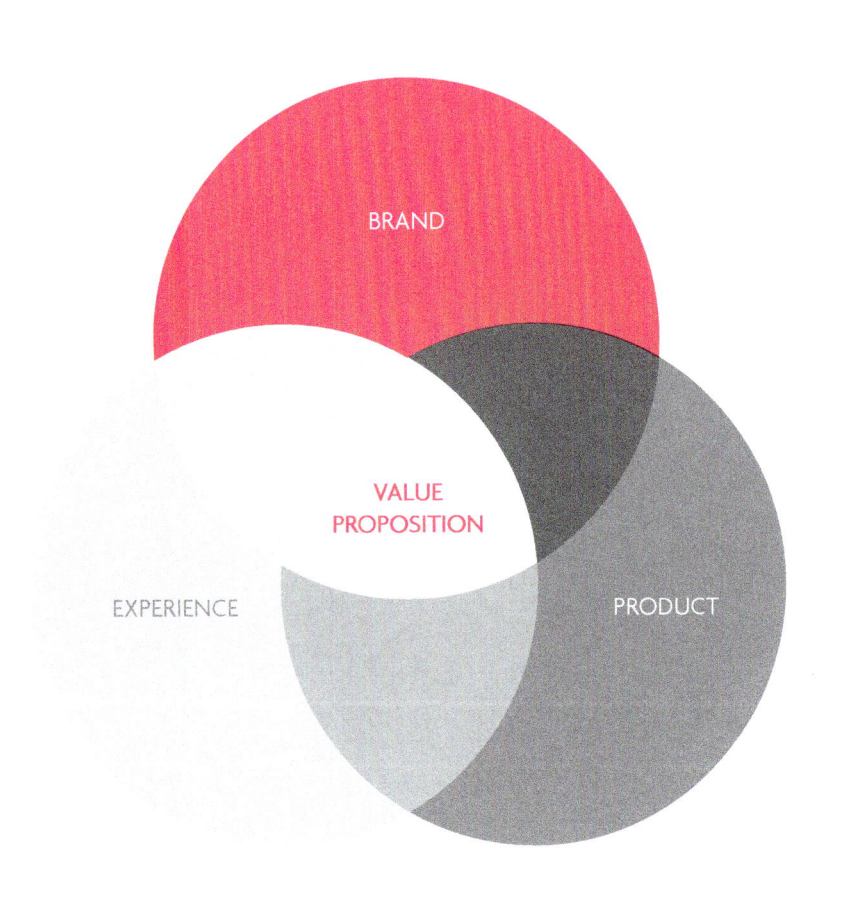

VALUE
PROPOSITION

EXPERIENCE

PRODUCT

VALUE PROPOSITION

Putting some time into creating your Value Proposition is well worth the effort and investment.

Your value proposition **tells potential customers** why they should do business with you rather than your competitors and makes the **benefits** of your products or services crystal clear to your potential customers.

How does your product or service help **solve** a customer's problem?

You Value Proposition is a sentence or paragraph that clearly articulates:
- What your services, business, or organisation does
- Who it brings value to
- Why it's valuable for those people

You need to **think** about your value proposition from two sides:

First, the experiences of your customers and second, the capabilities of your product or service.

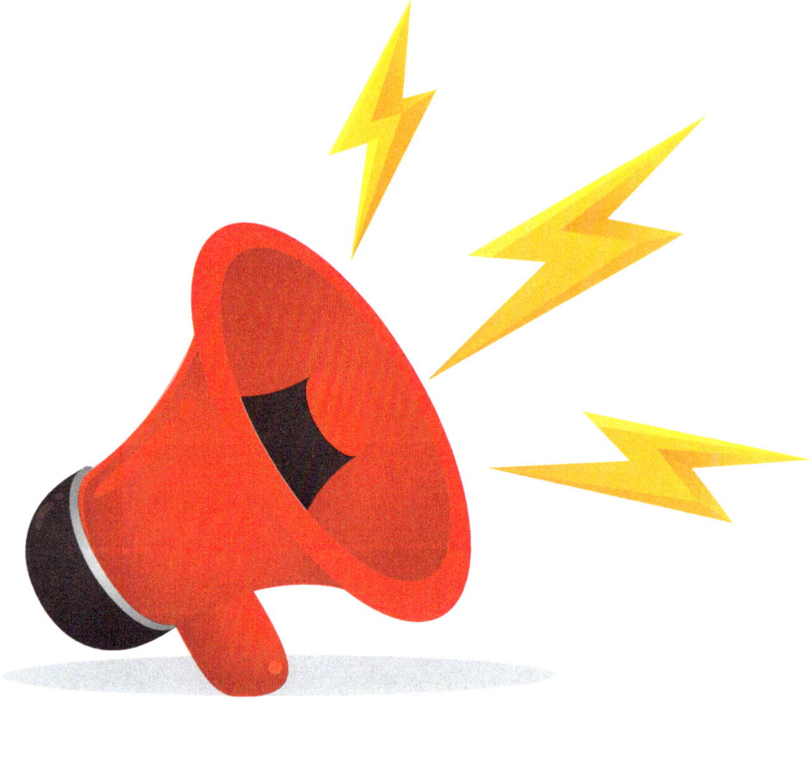

YOUR POTENTIAL CUSTOMERS

TARGET MARKET

Your target market is a group of people that your product or service is intended for. They are the group that you are marketing your product or service towards, to create more **awareness** about it.

How to define your target market:
- Look at your current customers. Why do they buy from you?
- Check out your competition
- Think about what problems your product or service solves

For example, my target market is **growing businesses** who want to build and market their brand more effectively.

Who is your target market and why?

_____
_____
_____
_____
_____
_____
_____
_____

TARGET AUDIENCE

Your target audience should be the customers that you have narrowed down to from your target market. This helps you to **be specific** when creating your value proposition message, so it **relates** to this audience.

Being specific about your target audience will mean that you are marketing your product or service to the **right people**.

DESCRIBE YOUR TARGET AUDIENCE

IDEAL CUSTOMER

We looked at this earlier, this is where that work comes to fruition. Check back to **pg. 46**, have you created your Ideal Customer profiles? Have you named them and given them a face?

YOUR PRODUCT OR SERVICE

What is your product or service?

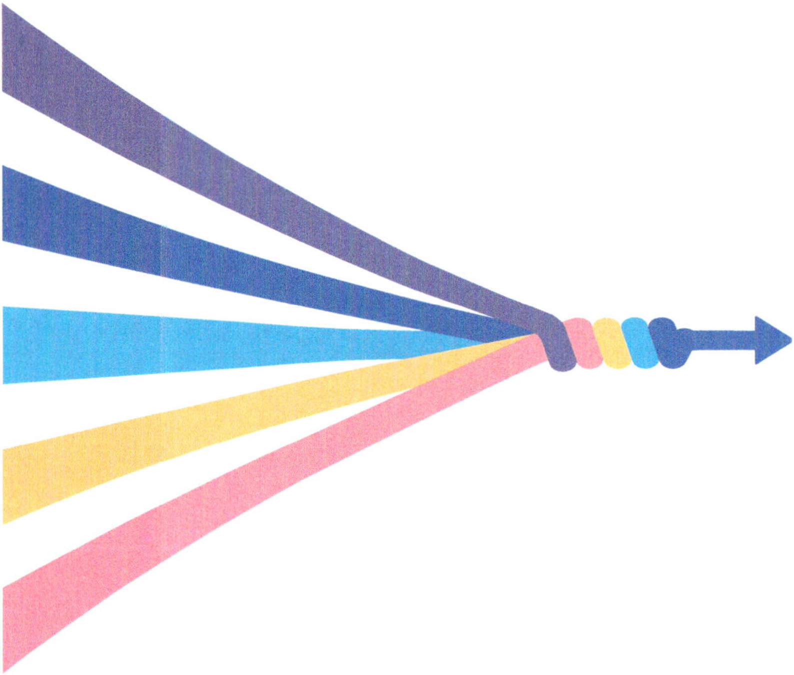

THE FAB FRAMEWORK
(Features, Advantages, and Benefits)

TARGET MARKET

The FAB Framework is a simple but effective tool to help you communicate (and market) the major aspects of your business. It becomes the basis for all your communication to current and potential customers. It is based on describing your key products or services in terms of Feature, Advantage and Benefit (FAB) and can be used by you and your team to break down your **key value points** into components to communicate them effectively.

FEATURE-ADVANTAGE-BENEFIT

You will also notice that each value point is divided into a feature followed by an advantage followed by **the end benefit**. This structure is designed to:

1. Highlight the key feature (characteristic or attribute)
2. Provide some descriptive explanation of why the feature is good or how the feature works (i.e., the advantage)
3. Describe the end benefit of the feature to each customer profile - you may have several for your different products or services.

Feature	Advantage	Benefit

BENEFITS: THE "SO WHAT?!" TEST

If you are talking to a potential customer and they say (or maybe just think) "**So What?!**", then the chances are you are talking about features, not benefits.

It's a trap we can all easily fall into. We are enthusiastic about our businesses and want to tell people about what we do and how we do it, to produce products or services – and forget to sell the **customer benefits**.

The customer will ask themselves "**What's in it for me?**" and if we fail to **explain** what's in it for them (customer benefits), and just talk about the facts or features of the product or service, they will walk away.

EXAMPLE: To define a benefit you ask yourself So what?

> The oven preheats quickly.
> So what?
>
> It's quickly ready to start cooking your dinner.
> So what?
>
> Your food is on the table sooner.
> So what?

Life is less stressful. There's less hanging around the kitchen waiting for the oven to get ready. And you don't have to worry you might forget to preheat your oven.

MORE EXAMPLES OF THE SO WHAT? HACK

The So what? Hack works in any industry:
Our doors have strong hinges.
So what? They won't bend when the door is slammed shut a thousand times.

We monitor your servers.
So what? Your servers won't go down, so you and your staff can continue working.

I write high-converting web copy.
So what? You can convert more web visitors into leads and business.

Read through your website or marketing content and ask for each statement: So what? **Keep asking So what?** If you can get to five for each statement, you'll find the real benefits.

BRING IT ALL TOGETHER

Value Proposition formulas
Geoff Moore's Value propositioning framework
The framework asks five questions:
1. Who is your company, product, or service for?
2. What challenges are they facing?
3. What is your product name?
4. What is your product category?
5. What is the benefit your product offers?

Template:

> For _____ (target customer) who _____
> (state the need or opportunity) our (product / service name) is
> _____ (product category)
> that (statement of benefit) _____.

Then, we put all of that into words like this example:

For non-technical marketers *who* struggle to find return on investment in social media *our* product is web-based analytics software *that* translates engagement metrics into actionable revenue metrics.

High concept pitch template
This value proposition template comes from Venture Hacks. This one's a simple concept. You take an existing successful company that's disrupt-ted their industry — Tesla, for example.

Then, determine the term that best describes your business sector — if you're in PR, you might choose the term "communications." So, your value proposition would be "Tesla of communications."

The idea behind this value proposition framework is that you're leveraging the success of the business you're referencing, thereby implying that your intention is to follow a similar path.

Template:

(Proven industry example) for/of (new sector)

For example:
1. YouTube: "Flickr for video"
2. Backdraft (Movie): Top Gun in a firehouse
3. Dogland: Disneyland for dogs

Steve Blank's XYZ framework
This is the simplest of the three frameworks — we help X do Y by doing Z, where X is your target audience, Y is the goal or problem they want to solve, and Z is the method by which you achieve it.

For example:
We help people without 3D printers (X) bring their ideas to life (Y) **by** providing 3D printing services and a marketplace **for** 3D printed products (Z)

Ad-Lib Value Proposition Template

Strategyzer's Ad-libs are a great way to quickly shape alternative directions for your value proposition. They force you to pinpoint how exactly you are going to creating value. Work up three to five different directions by filling out the blanks in the ad-lib below.

> Our _____ (Products an services)
> Help(s) _____ (customer segment)
> Who want to (achieve)
> By _____ (reducing, avoiding, customer pain)
> And _____ (increasing or enabling, customer gain).

WHAT IS A GOOD VALUE PROPOSITION STATEMENT?

A good value proposition statement speaks to the **challenges** your target audience is facing and concisely **explains** how your company helps **solve** those challenges.

For example:

    Amazon – "Fast delivery, convenience, choice, low prices."
    Uber – "The Smartest Way to Get Around"
    Apple iPhone – "The Experience IS the Product"

01
02
03

BRAND IDENTITY

LOGO

LOGO MEANING AND STORY

Your logo is the most visible and recognisable part of your brand, and it is the **cornerstone** of your brand identity... more about that later. Your logo should have meaning, it can represent you, what you or your business does, or the name of your business.

Picture Aladdin's lamp – this fairy tale icon is a global symbol that instantly **brings a story to mind**, be it Aladdin himself, the genie, or the three wishes this symbol brings to mind.

My business for example is called 'Make a brew' – what on earth made me call the company 'Make a Brew' After all I'm a branding expert not a café!

It's simple really. I'm from Yorkshire in the North of England, so when I meet my customers, whether virtually or in person, I make a brew and we sit and have a chat about their requirements. It's a much better way for us to discover all we need to about one another than being all formal and stuffy! For me, it's all about **good conversation** and **making a connection**. Great ideas spring from good conversation.

(Just as a point of reference, if you're not northern, or indeed from the UK, then a brew is a cup of tea... don't want you thinking I brew my own beer or gin or something...)

So, the logo is made up of three mugs viewed from the top to represent **meeting**, **conversation**, **collaboration**, and **working together**.

Other logo stories...

Apple is one of the most iconic brands out there with its instantly recognisable apple-shaped logo plastered across its range of products. But there is an interesting story behind the famous fruit logo. It hasn't always been the famous bitten Apple we know and love today. Originally it was first fronted by a hand-drawn detailed logo featuring Issac Newton sitting under a tree – depicting the famous illustration of the law of gravity.

The iconic bitten apple that we see today has been around since 1977, Rob Janoff designed it like a half-eaten apple to demonstrate **scale**. This enabled the users to know that it is an apple and not a tomato or cherry.

Another reason for such a design according to Rob was to reflect that it was something **everyone could experience**, like taking a bite of an apple.

The famous McDonald's Logo from North America and the Middle East to Europe and beyond, McDonald's restaurant 'golden arches' logo can be easily recognised by anyone from any geographic background.

The McDonald's logo is symbolic of the golden arches that were part of the architecture of the first franchised restaurant in 1952.

After Ray Kroc took over the business in 1961, he incorporated the two arches to form the new McDonald's logo that looked like the letter "M".

McDonald's logo design is one of the most popular emblems in modern history.

It looks equally amazing on every surface whether it is a neon-sign board, vinyl banner, or a computer screen.

Its **memorable design** easily retains in your memory.

You can quickly **identify** those arches even from a long distance.

> The strongest logos tell simple stories.

———— Sol Sender

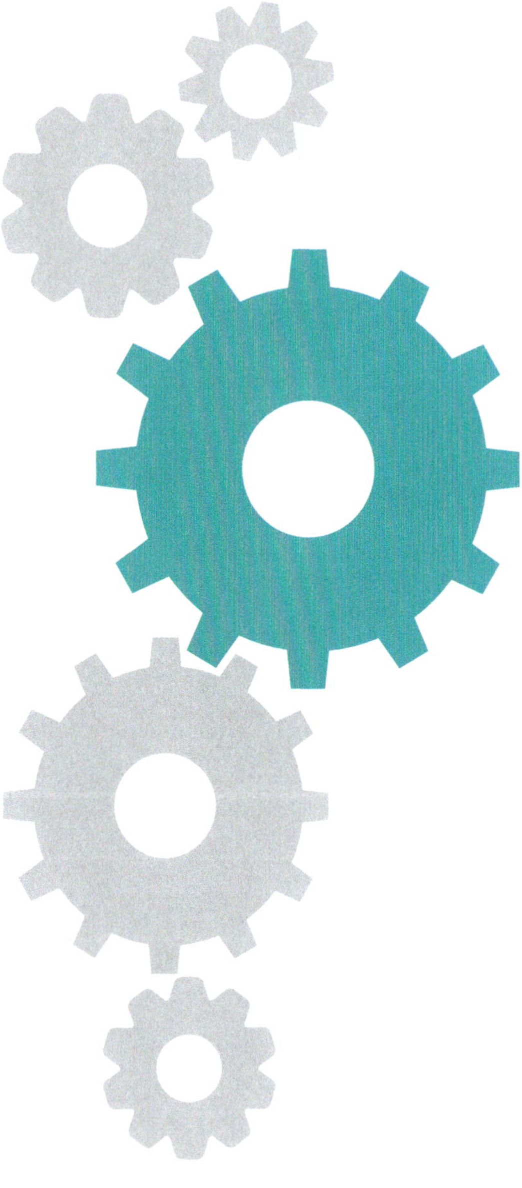

BRAND IDENTITY SYSTEM

When brand identity is mentioned, most people tend to think of the logo design. While a logo is one of the most important elements of a brand identity, there are other elements that are just as important and perhaps sometimes even more so.

WHAT IS A BRAND IDENTITY SYSTEM?

A Brand Identity System is a collection of elements that work together to **create unified**, **consistent**, and **flexible** brand assets that communicate the brand value to the target audience effectively.

This collection of elements is made up of six major brand assets including the primary logo, secondary logo, colour palette, typography, visual brand assets (including brand pattern, iconography etc), and brand tone (which includes visual image and photo standards as well as the tone of voice in all messaging and communications) all of which help to create and awesome brand.

Primary Logo

The first and the most visible symbol of brand power is the primary logo. It should be as simple as possible and lean towards conceptual and abstract visual elements rather than literally trying to show what your brand does or stands for.

The primary logo should be flexible enough to work well on and off line and at all sizes, make sure it's going to be legible as a social media profile image when viewed on mobile. It should be **easy to reproduce** and must use solid design principles.

A good logo design should have these six qualities:

- The logo should be scalable
- In most cases, the logo should have solid colours
- The logo should be adaptable
- The logo should be memorable
- The logo should be unique and
- The logo should be on message

Secondary Logo

For many, the idea of a secondary logo may be alien. In fact, the golden rule of branding was to have one single logo that was **consistent** across all media. But the landscape has changed now and so has the definition of a brand identity.

Everyone is a publisher these days with their own publishing channels such as blogs social media, websites, etc. The Internet has become a noisy and chaotic environment where information is provided at a lightning-fast pace.

In such an environment, how is a brand to stand out and thrive? This is where the secondary logo comes into play. It **supports** the primary logo and is used on secondary touch points such as merchandising, marketing materials, social media campaigns and more.

For lifestyle brands such as clothing and fashions brands, a secondary logo serves a supremely important role. It is used on **touch points** such as labels, tags, etc

RED
Excitement, Strength, Love, Energy

ORANGE
Confidence, Success, Bravery, Sociability

YELLOW
Creativity, Happiness, Warmth, Cheer

GREEN
Nature, Healing, Freshness, Quality

BLUE
Trust, Peace, Loyalty, Competence

PURPLE
Royalty, Luxury, Spirituality, Ambition

PINK
Compassion, Sincerity, Sweet Sophistication,

BROWN
Dependable, Rugged, Trustworthy, Simple

BLACK
Formality, Dramatic, Sophistication, Security

WHITE
Clean, Simplicity, Innocence, Honest

Colour Palette

Most brands have a signature colour scheme, whether it is black and white or a more creative palette. However, many companies think that their carefully chosen colours are limited to their letterhead, logo, and signs. Using your colours **throughout your business** will give a better-rounded experience to people who interact with your business while helping to make those colours synonymous with your brand. For example, you might wear a particular colour for the majority of time – for me that's blue, navy specifically, so incorporating that into your brand identity colours can help you **'look on-brand'** naturally.

Owning a colour in your market segment should be one of the goals of your branding – 'JCB Yellow' for example. If used strategically, you can own a colour which your target audience come to associate with your brand. At times, this can be so effective that just the colour will remind people of your brand without the primary or secondary logos visible.

When choosing colours for your brand, base them on their suitability to your brand along with ensuring they align with the world view of your target audience. One of the examples I use here is you wouldn't associate fire engine red with a funeral director, but that's not to say a funeral director couldn't use a shade of red, something like a claret wine red could work quite nicely.

Abc

Serif typeface

Abc

Sans-Serif typeface

Typography

Typography is fundamental part of establishing a solid brand identity system. Selecting the right fonts to represent your brand could be a daunting process and most brands simply make random choices based on personal preferences.

Typefaces have **personality** and you should try and identify typography that matches the personality of your brand. Different types evoke different **feelings**. For example, typically serif typefaces represent **tradition** while sans-serif ones are more **modern**. Some fonts look **friendly** while other look **corporate**.

Think about **readability** too – some fonts are harder to read than others when on screens or different coloured backgrounds for example white text on a yellow background is hard to read on paper but almost impossible on screen.

White text on a yellow background

Black text on a yellow background

Serif formats are good for print like newspapers and articles and sans serif fonts are easier to read on screens, on websites or social media platforms.

As with colours, your brand should have a primary typeface which is usually used in your primary brand logo. Unless you have a custom typeface in your logo design, you can also use the primary typeface for headlines and other important messages of your brand.

You should use this primary font sparingly so that you do not dilute the primary brand logo. Secondary and tertiary typefaces should **complement** the primary typography.

For example:

Headings

Subheadings

Content

> Your choice of typeface is as important as what you do with it.
>
> —— Bonnie Siegler

Helping you *get stuff done* and giving you time to *do your thing*

www.pippamell.com

Visual Brand Extensions

Visual brand extensions are design elements that support and enhance the brand's visual **experience**. These could be things such as the official brand pattern or icons.

Having an official brand pattern that is used as subtle part of the brand's visual makeup can create a **lasting memory** or your brand.

Iconography can be another powerful part of your **brand's toolkit**. Custom icons created specifically for your brand can establish a direct subconscious **connection** with your target audience.

For example:

Using logos and brand marks as repeating patterns for social media banners or, to create interest on business cards.

" Personality is critical to success - for brands as well as people. Don't leave it to chance

———— Sir Richard Branson

Brand Tone

Finally, one of the most important brand assets is your brand tone. A brand tone is the **personality of your brand**. This is the **impression** or perception that you want your brand to convey when interacting with people.

A brand tone is what your brand says but more importantly it is said. Good messages take your competitive positioning and brand strategy to the next level. They hone in on what's **important** to your market and **communicate it consistently** and effectively. How you respond when asked about your brand or service or product and the tone of your messaging has a **huge impact** on how your brand is perceived by your target audience.

Your Brand tone can manifest in the following ways:
- Brand elevator pitch
- Positioning statements
- Vision and mission statements
- Brand's tagline and slogan
- Press releases
- Social media content
- Blog posts and articles
- Communication style – via email, phone, or face to face

18

CONSISTENCY IS KEY

WHAT IS BRAND CONSISTENCY (AND WHY DOES IT MATTER)?

Brand consistency is the practice of always **delivering messages** aligned with the core brand values in the **same** tone, presenting the brand logo in a similar way, and **repeating** the same colours throughout your visual brand elements. Over time, these elements become etched in the minds of customers, and they're more likely to **remember** your brand. Brand consistency also ensures that your brand is easily recognizable across marketing channels and **touch points**.

It's not just about the visual elements of a brand, though. There are three critical areas where brands must be consistent to drive customer loyalty:

- **Customer Experience** – Providing a consistent customer experience builds trust and confidence in your brand.
- **Values** – Back up your words with actions.
- **Brand Identity Elements** – These are the visual brand components that make your brand recognisable and help you stand out from the competition.

BENEFITS OF BRAND CONSISTENCY

The most obvious benefit of brand consistency is brand **recognition**. Every business should strive to be immediately recognisable by their target audience. Not only does it help to build a strong association between your core messages and values and the visual elements of your brand, but it also **sets your brand apart** from the competition – a particularly valuable perk in highly competitive, saturated markets.

Other benefits of brand consistency include:

Shaping brand perception
When you have brand consistency in your corner, shaping the perception of your brand in the minds of customers is more easily achieved by introducing key messages alongside your consistent brand elements.

Evoking positive emotions
When you tie brand consistency to positive emotions (through carefully-crafted words and imagery), your audience will begin to associate those positive emotions with your brand. When done right, those emotions are eventually evoked with exposure to a stand-alone logo or your brand name, whether or not those positive emotion-evoking messages and images are present. That means more exposure to your brand can make people feel happy, and happy people are more likely to buy (especially from a company they trust).

Building trust and loyalty
Speaking of trust, brand consistency leads to confidence among customers that they'll have a certain experience when they engage with your brand. One often-cited example is Coca-Cola, a beverage brand with worldwide recognition. No one ever wonders what a

bottle of Coca-Cola will taste like, because brand consistency ensures that it's always the same. Remember: brand consistency is as much about the customer experience as it is about the visuals.

Differentiating your brand
Brand consistency is a key factor in differentiation, as well. In a competitive landscape with a variety of similar offerings, brand consistency often means the difference between earning a customer's business or losing them to the competition. Leverage brand consistency to communicate, again and again, what it is that sets your company apart from the rest.

BEST PRACTICES FOR BRAND CONSISTENCY
How do the world's most recognizable brands establish and maintain brand consistency? **It takes time** but following a few key best practices will keep you on the right path.

USE CAUTION WHEN RE BRANDING
While the idea of re branding your business might seem exciting, always consider the impact on brand consistency. If you haven't already established distinctive brand assets, re branding may be feasible without sacrificing some hard-earned brand recognition. If your visual elements are already established distinctive assets with strong brand associations, it's still possible to re brand – but do so with caution and try to maintain some core elements of your old identity to ease the transition.

IF IT'S BORING, YOU'RE DOING IT RIGHT

If you get bored looking at the same visual elements, the same layouts, and using the same colour schemes or fonts for your marketing materials, you're on the right track. If you are working on your own design and marketing materials day after day, it tends to get a bit boring – but that means it's more likely to establish **brand recognition** in the minds of your target customers.

USE A BRAND STYLE GUIDE

There are so many elements that make up a brand and ensuring consistency across everyone is a daunting task. **Create a brand style guide** to define your brand elements and branding rules to keep everyone on the same page and your materials and messaging on-brand. Your brand style guide should include your company's mission, the brand's colour palette, fonts (including when and how they're used, such as for certain headings, etc.), brand voice and copy guidelines, photo and imagery styles, and any other information that your team or suppliers need to know to **maintain consistency**.

> If content is king, consistency is queen.

—— Clare Froggatt

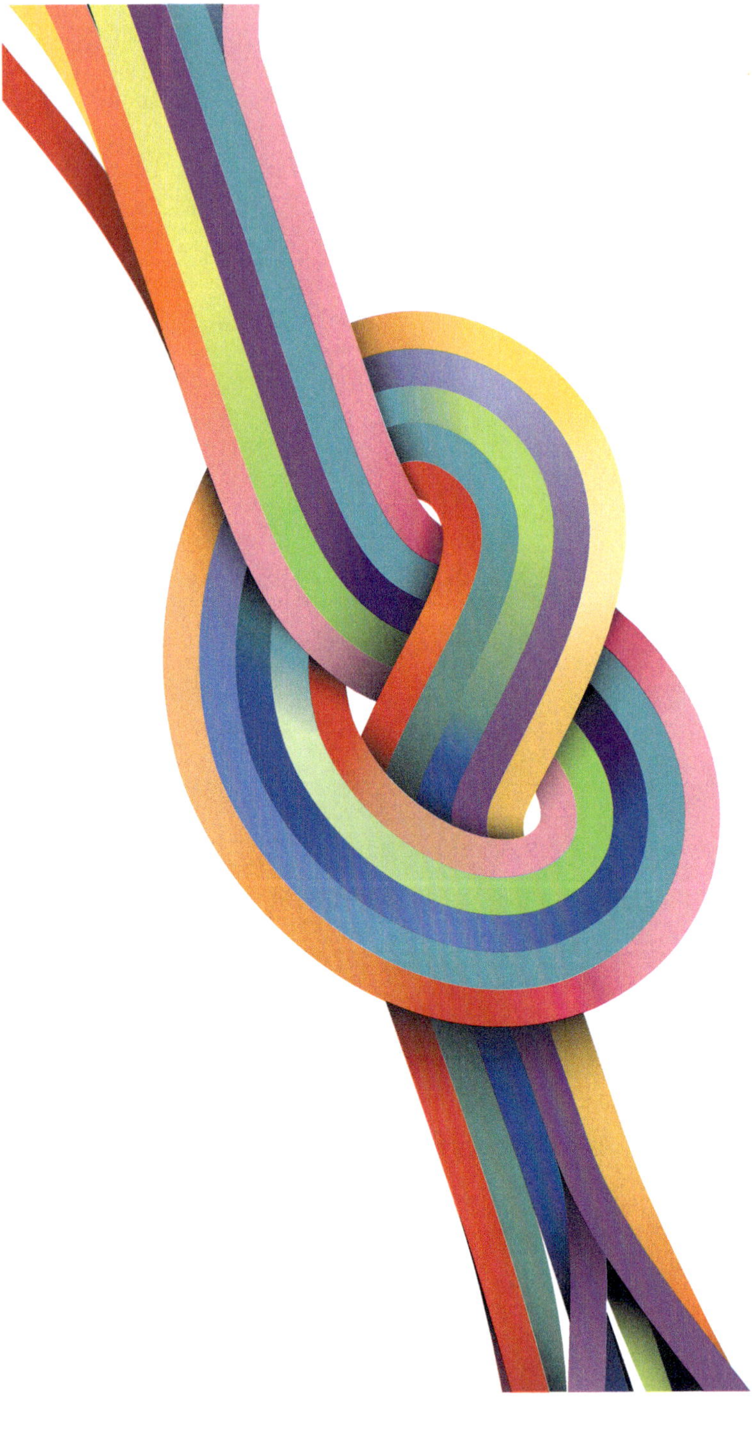

NEED MORE HELP?

Don't tie yourself in knots, book a Brand #Boom session and I will help you get unstuck or help you to implement Branding 3x3 into your business.

BRAND #BOOM...
...an idea generating, strategic, action plan

Step One: 15 Minute Discovery Call
We quickly get to know one another, discuss where you're currently at, what you're struggling with, and where you'd like to be.

If we both feel like a good fit – we book a 90-minute strategy session so I can help you achieve your goals.

Step Two: 90-minute strategy and ideas session (delivered on zoom or in person, location dependent)
Following the meeting you will receive a detailed, written, action plan so that you have a clear record of what actions you need to implement. If the meeting was held on Zoom you will also receive a recording of the meeting.

Step Three: A 30-minute accountability, follow up call

A week or two after our strategy session, we'll jump on a call to see how you're getting on. I can clarify anything you're unsure of and make sure you're taking the action we agreed to move your brand and business to the next level.

Call: 0114 3999 819
Email clare@makeabrew.co.uk

GLOSSARY

BRAND-RELATED TERMS
Brand
The term "brand" has two meanings. First, it refers to one subset of a larger corporation (e.g. Sprite is a brand of the Coca-Cola Company). It also refers to the perception that people have about a company or its products. This perception can come from a variety of sources, including firsthand experience, word of mouth, advertising, and other brand expressions (logo, colour scheme, writing style, etc.) Essentially, a brand is what people think about your business. And while it's not a tangible thing, it's one of the most important things to consider when running a business because it helps create customer loyalty and allows your business stand apart from the competition.

For Example: Coca-Cola's brand is about inspiring optimism and happiness across the globe. Everything they do from community service to advertising helps to build that perception.

Brand asset
A brand asset is used to identify your company. Often, these are images, logos or words that tie directly to your business. For example, the Nike "swoosh" and the tagline "Just do it" are both brand assets of Nike. It's important to keep your brand assets organized and easy to access – you never know when that big break will come and you'll need to send a high-resolution image of your logo.

Brand positioning

Brand positioning, like many of these terms, contains the definition right in the term. It's how a company chooses to position itself within a given industry to help it stand apart from the competition. Good brand positioning consists of three basic parts:

- Target audience: Who is the brand for? (Men, women, professionals, creative types, etc.)
- Benefit: How will the company make the audience's life better? What's in it for them? (Peace of mind, save money, look/feel better, etc.)
- Differentiator: Why choose this brand over others in the industry? (Previous experience, advanced technology, superior design, etc.)

For example, Apple positions its brand to create an emotional connection with its customers through exceptional experiences is an excellent approach, especially in this competitive industry. In the same manner, Apple uses its positioning approach based on competition. Since competition is tight in the technology industry, Apple ensures to continuously invest in R&D and introduce innovative products and features all the time. It keeps on making unique technologies for the brand and cannot be copied anywhere else.

There's an unlimited number of ways you could position yourself against the competition, but it's important to pick out what your business's strengths are and focus on those.

Branding

Branding is the action that you take to separate your business from everyone else's. You can do this by applying visual and/or audio cues to products, services and other places where people interact with your brand (packaging, website, shop layouts, commercials, printed materials, etc.). For example, a can of pop takes on a much different meaning when it has the Coca-Cola branding on it as opposed to your local supermarket's branding.

DESIGN-RELATED TERMS
Now that we've discussed some branding terms, let's get into the details of your brand's design.

Colour palette

This is the main set of colours that a business uses. The most obvious example of a colour palette comes from UPS, who even makes mention of it in their tagline "What can Brown do for you?" Many businesses hold trademarks on certain colours in order to distinguish themselves in their industry, like Cadbury Purple and 3M Canary Yellow (Post-it notes).

Logo

Your logo is the mark that represents your business. You know the iconic ones: the McDonald's golden arches, or the Nike swoosh. Logos can be comprised of any combination of graphics, images and words.

Visual identity

Your visual identity is the external expression of your brand. Your brand assets, combine to make up your visual identity. When branding, it's crucial to first determine what you want the perception of your business to be, so you can create a visual identity that gives off that perception. Many of the best businesses have a very coherent visual identity – one where everything that the company produces is similar in its look and feel.

OTHER DESIGN-RELATED TERMS

Here are some terms that you might not be familiar with, though they'll certainly come in handy when thinking about building your brand.

Pixel

A pixel (short for "picture element") is the smallest individual part of an image or graphic when viewed on an electronic screen, like a computer or TV. The more pixels that an image has, the better it will be able to represent the image, because the higher number of pixels will allow for more detail. The number of pixels in an image is often called the "resolution" of the image.

PPI and DPI

These two acronyms refer to Pixels Per Inch and Dots Per Inch, respectively. These terms have different meanings depending on what they're referring to. When discussing an image, PPI refers to the number of pixels per inch in the image. However, when discussing an output for the image (such as a printed page, computer monitor, digital camera image sensor or TV screen), the terms differ. PPI measures the number of pixels per inch available on the electronic outputs, and DPI measures the number of dots per inch that a printer can print onto a physical page. Generally speaking, images with more pixels per inch are good, as they will be a higher quality image when printed.

Raster vs. vector
These two terms refer to graphics – raster graphics (sometimes called bitmaps) are images where the colours and lines are represented as points on a rectangular grid. If you enlarge a raster graphic, it gets "pixelated," I refer to this as looking like Lego, which means you can see where the individual points are in the original image. These are usually saved in forms like .jpg, .gif, and .png. Vector graphics are the opposite of raster graphics, in that they can be shrunk or enlarged indefinitely without losing their sharpness at any size. Vector files are usually saved as .ai, .eps or .pdf form.

Scalable
Most often used to describe an image or logo, this term refers directly back to the discussion of raster vs. vector. Scalable means that the image or graphic you're using looks good at any size, so it will be as recognizable and clear on a stamp or a banner on a skyscraper. In order to make your images scalable, they should most likely be in vector format, or at least have a very high PPI number.

PRINT-RELATED TERMS

When promoting your brand, you'll need to translate it to your marketing materials. This is where the fun begins, but it's important to know a few terms from the printing world to ensure you successfully navigate the designing and printing stages.

Bleed line

This is the very edge of the product that you're creating. If your product has a background image or colour that you want to extend all the way to the edge, make sure that it goes right up to the bleed line to avoid any potential white space after the product is cut by the printer.

Safety line

Remember when you were a kid and you were told to colour inside the lines? This is the adult version of that. This line marks the point at which your product (business cards, postcards, flyers etc.) might get cut, so make sure everything that you want printed stays fully inside this safety line.

Trim area

This is the area between the safety line and the bleed line. Due to tiny imperfections in printing processes, this small area of your product is where the cut will occur.

TYPOGRAPHY - FONT-RELATED TERMS

Serif

Serifs are the small lines and hooks at the end of the strokes in some letters.

Sans serif
Sans means "without." A sans serif font has no serifs.

Script
Script typefaces use a flowing, cursive stroke.

Slab serif
Slab serif is distinguished by thick, block-like serifs.

Font spacing
The vertical and horizontal spacing of a font is often altered to change its appearance.

Kerning
Kerning is the adjustment of space between pairs of letters in the same word. Certain pairs of letters create awkward spaces, and kerning adds or subtracts space between them to create more visually appealing and readable text.

Leading
Pronounced "ledding," leading (also known as line-height) is the space between two lines of text.

Tracking
Not to be confused with kerning, tracking is the adjustment of space for groups of letters and entire blocks of text. Tracking affects every character in the selected text and is used to change its overall appearance.

Font case

Typically, characters are available in two forms.

Uppercase

The large, capital letters of a typeface are UPPERCASE. They're also used to emphasise point or create a certain tone or emotion.

Lowercase

Lowercase refers to the small letters of a typeface.

Small caps

SMALL CAPS—or small capitals—are uppercase characters that are the same height as lowercase letters. They are used to prevent capitalized words from appearing too large on the page. Want an example? Open just about any book and look at the opening words of a chapter.

Font style

Beyond spacing and case, fonts can also be altered by scale, weight and style.

Point size

Point size is the size of text. There are approximately 72 (72.272) points in one inch.

Font weight

Font weight specifies the **boldness** of a font.

Italics

When characters slope to the right, they're in *italics*, a visual technique used to draw attention to specific words or sentences within a paragraph.

COLOUR

Colour theory

Colour theory is used to explore the best types of colours to work in different design instances—for example, choosing a pastel scheme for a website that needs to feel soft, or picking red and yellow for a magazine ad that needs to evoke energy.

Hue, tint, tone and shade

Hue is pure colour. Tint is a hue with white added. Tone is a hue with grey added. Shade is a hue with black added.

Saturation

Saturation is defined by the intensity of colour.

Palette

A palette is the range of colours used in a design. These are colours that work well together and are often aesthetically pleasing. Designers will defines a palette for a project to create consistency and evoke a specific feeling.

Warm and cool colours

Warm colours can be found on one half of the colour wheel (reds, oranges, yellows and pinks). Cool colours occupy the other half (blues, greens and purples).

Gradient
Gradient is a gradual change from one colour to another. (For example, blue transitioning gradually to green).

Opacity
Opacity is synonymous with non-transparency. The more transparent an image, the lower its opacity.

CMYK
CMYK is a 4-colour printing process made up of cyan, magenta, yellow and key (black). CMYK colours in print will never appear as vibrant as RGB colours on screen because CMYK creates colour by adding colour together (making images darker) while RGB colours come from light.

RGB
RGB stands for red, green and blue, the three colours of light typically used to display images on a digital screen.

Pantone
Developed by Pantone Corporation, a professional colour company, Pantone is the most widely used, proprietary colour system for blending colours. The system includes colours that cannot be mixed in CMYK.

WEB & DIGITAL
Web page elements
Most web page designs include combination of these elements.

Header
Design elements repeated at the top of every page is called a header.

Navigation & navigation bar
Navigation is a road-map to the most important parts of a website and should be visually consistent across all pages. A navigation bar is a set of links repeated on each page that often includes links to pages like "About us", "Products," "Contact us" and "Testimonials."

Breadcrumb trail
Breadcrumbs are navigation elements that generally appear near the top of a page to show users the section hierarchy of the current page.

Body text
Body text is the main written content of a page.

Links
Any word or an image can be a link that can take users to another page.

Sidebar
A sidebar is the left or right-hand column of a page typically used for either vertical navigation links or advertising. It may also contain site search, subscription links (RSS, newsletters, etc.) or social network buttons.

Banner
Typically located at the top of a page or in a sidebar, banners are advertisements that link to other websites.

Footer
Design elements repeated at the bottom of every page is called a footer, extended menus for example including privacy policy and terms & conditions.

Landing page
A landing page is a single page that appears in response to search engine result. Landing pages are used for lead generation.

THE AUTHOR

Clare Froggatt, is a branding expert with over 25 years' experience in creating and building brands, and runs her branding agency Make a brew. She love's a good cup of tea and believes there's no better way to get a conversation started than over a good brew, as said in the North of England, in the UK.

She has worked for and with large organisations like the NHS and Coors Brewers, right down to small businesses, start-ups and sole traders. Make a brew is her third business in which she brings together a fun, authentic, creative and strategic approach when it comes to marketing - a rare combination.

Helping small businesses is her passion, She loves to simplify the many branding and marketing strategies and tactics that are out there to make it easy for smaller businesses to get results. She has extensive experience which covers every area of marketing from branding, design, websites, content, strategy, and launches.

It's that philosophy that inspired her to create Branding 3x3, which started out as a presentation to educate business owners on the three main elements of branding and the three key elements within each.

This book expands that presentation out into simple and relatable explanations and exercises.

Clare loves LEGO and describes it is a perfect way to demonstrate that building a brand as a step by step process.

ACKNOWLEDGMENTS

Claire Taylor – For proofreading & editing this book and for being my friend and business guide – Make a brew would not be where it is today without Claire.

Lisa East – Inspiring me to put this book together and being my podcast partner. Together we bring the creativity, madness and realism to podcasting.

John Froggatt - The 'grammar fascist' and my dad - the apple didn't fall far from the tree on the tech and geek stuff but I got the design rather than English skills.

Becky Jamieson - For helping me to build a better customer journey model into my business so I can talk to you from experience in this book.

And the last word...

#Boom

Printed in Great Britain
by Amazon